TALENT

Vs.

NEPOTISM

The Journey for Fame

By

Amarnath K. A

First published June 2020

Amazon Asia-Pacific Holdings Pvt. Ltd.

ISBN: 9798655730311

INTRODUCTION: The Idea

An idea can change your life as well as others'.

What I write in this book are my own little experiences. Through it, I intend to help you relate to them and take all the important notes and apply them to your life.

For those who don't know me, I'm Amarnath K. A, a 19-year-old Indian author from Kerala. Let's go straight to the topic.

It was one fine day during the time of corona, the worst pandemic witnessed by the world in the 21st century as of now. It had been a month since colleges were dismissed not only in Kerala but also all over India. My daily life as well as my friends' revolved fully around the Smartphone and social media. Then, something caught my attention; the celebrities in Instagram were posting their photos, and on the flipside, a lot of ordinary people were posting content which expressed their skills and talents. I wondered seeing the difference between the responses evoked by both these actions. I asked myself why there is such a glaring difference when celebrities show their skills and normal people like me show their talents. The question what I can do to make myself and others rise to their level made way into an Idea. Now I've gotten the answers to those questions and here, I am going to share my insights as a metaphorical story.

I would like to introduce you to the main protagonist of the story: Talent.

Talent was a young, determined man who did exceptionally well whatever he put his hand to. He was charming and quite popular among the folks. It was difficult to conquer his heart. Someone who had won his heart was called as talented. Those who came to be called as talented had won either one or more of his hearts since he had infinite hearts. People found him charismatic and hence, desirable, for his exceptional skills in music, dance, acting sports and whatnot.

Even when someone had won one of his hearts, they had to work very hard in order to be like him. There were also people who became quite good at something even when they didn't have his heart, provided they worked very hard with him.

One fine day, Talent saw the glimpse of a beautiful lady in the woods. As he went closer, her beauty began to shine as bright as the sun. But just like the sun, she was unreachable even though he walked non-stop up the mountains and down the valleys. Hours passed by. The sun began to set and so did her elegant view; she began to disappear. Exhausted from the long quest and desperate to find his love, he sat under a tree. Then, as if determined by the destiny, one of his beloved followers found him and gave him a map to the place where this beautiful lady, Talent's blind love, resides. He told Talent that at night, she is captivated in the Castle of Emperor Nepotism, and she can escape from his clutches only during the daytime. She awaits day and night, keeping herself alive in the hope of uniting with him one day when he would reach her with the help of the map as the Prophecy bestows.

Curious to know about her, Talent asked him what her name was, where the map leads to, and how he can defeat Nepotism who captures her every night. The beloved follower smiled and said "Her name is Fame and this map leads to her. You can defeat Nepotism, with your Heart. Only you. That is your destiny". Then the follower happily disappeared into the Abbey as he had fulfilled his duty of showing Talent the way to Fame in order to make the prophecy come true.

As Talent glanced at the map, he understood that the places depicted in the map were not actual places but symbols which stood for the things he had to do.

Talent saw 7 places in the map which he had to reach in order to unite with his love, Fame.

They were:

1. His Own Heart
2. The Mountain of Hearts
3. The City of Heartless where to share his heart
4. The Top of the Mountain of heart
5. The Sword of Press which he had to Wield
6. The Land of Press which he had to Conquer
7. The Land of Wiki which has to be conquered with the Army of Press
8. Fame's Day Castle

So, I'll be explaining each destination in detail, later. If you want to go right to the core idea of this book in relation to the story of Talent, go to chapter 1.

Let's come back to the real world for a better understanding.

This may seem very simple but trust me; I've worked day and night and have gone through hundreds of trials and errors to give you this information.

First things first. Let's focus on the Internal Conflict about the issue Inequality of Opportunity and Nepotism that pertains in our society. I know many of my friends (who like me are still teenagers) may find this too dry for their age. But the understanding is worth it which is why I'm writing this book.

There are two main reasons for a person's talent to be not seen/accepted/honoured before the public or the society:

1. Less opportunities/knowledge for those who are talented yet are from financially backward classes.

2. Nepotism or Favouritism of the existing people in their concerned field.

Firstly, let's focus on how people who have less opportunities/knowledge struggle in general.

The most common thing that ordinary people do is to present their talent through social media platforms like Instagram, Facebook, YouTube, Tiktok, twitter and so on. The one thing they don't know is that even if it reaches thousands of people virtually, in the real world, the society doesn't care. If there was a like button in newspapers, everyone would understand it for sure. Society as well as the public sees mainstream media as their Holy book of truth. No matter how much talent a person has got, he will not be accepted until basic local newspapers or their online websites write about him or his work. I have written exactly how to do that in the following chapters. You won't get a news report just because you have a talent. They need a story and you have to provide it. If I don't have a story, I won't get it too.

Another way through which common people present their talent is the competitions conducted by communities which also face the same fate unless it is conducted by an established organisation and is eventually chosen by the mainstream media.

So, is it wrong to use mainstream media to promote your talent?

The answer is both Yes and No.

It is a No, when your talent is used genuinely for the benefit of others or for any social cause.

It is a Yes, when it is used ONLY for your own personal interest unless you have achieved some recognition on a global or national level platform.

That's all about how normal people struggle with opportunity to present their talents before the public.

Secondly, we can have a look at how various sources show nepotism and favouritism as a reality.

"Nepotism is the favouritism shown on the basis of family relationship, as in business or politics "- Dictionary.com

If you search for Nepotism in India on internet, you can find something like this:

Corruption goes hand in hand with nepotism in India. It goes on in government and private jobs both. Nepotism is common in politics, judiciary, business and in the film industry. It goes on even in religious circles, arts, industry, and other types of organizations. Many members of Parliament and various Legislative Assemblies have a generations-long legacy of nepotic allocation of constituencies to their relatives.

Many judges and advocates of the High courts and the Supreme Court are alleged to be appointed by exercising casteism, nepotism and favouritism, primarily because the Supreme Court and the High Courts uses a non-transparent undemocratic appointment process called Collegium which recommends to the President, in a legally binding manner, the names of judges to be appointed or promoted to the higher judiciary. The various judicial services exams are also infamous for these practices.

 The Bajaj family is related to the Birla family which itself is related to the Biyani family by marriage. The Kapoor families, and many other Indian movie actors have brought their children into the movie industry with their endorsements and influence. Moreover, dynasty in politics remains. Rahul Gandhi, Vice-President of the Indian National Congress party, is a descendent of Jawaharlal Nehru and Indira Gandhi & Rajiv Gandhi. Data shows since 1999, the Congress has had 36 dynastic MPs elected to the Lok Sabha, with the BJP not far behind with 31 dynastic MPs.

The highly popular sport of cricket is also affected with nepotism, although to a lesser extent, in the form of Stuart Binny, Rohan Gavaskar and very recently Sachin Tendulkar. Home minister Amit Shah's son was appointed as the BCCI secretary.

But don't start to judge fast, let's put ourselves in their shoes. If you really wanted to be a musician, and your dad is a famous musician too, It is likely that he will do whatever is necessary to promote you in the field. It is something normal and I believe that no one should be harassed just because their predecessor happens to be in that field. The problem comes when people with more talent gets marginalised in the process and those with less talent in the field is forced into it because of the so called Legacy of the family which leads to the loss of Opportunity for others to grow.

<u>Chapter 1: Identifying Talent /His Own Heart.</u>

"Some people want it to happen, some wish it would happen, others make it happen." – Michael Jordan

Talent began searching for his real heart in a vast treasury of infinite hearts which was inside him. But how would he know which the right one was. He asked many of his followers but they always pointed at something which he was unsure of. He ran scientific tests to determine the true heart. But he was unsuccessful. He began to feel that his journey has ended even before he could begin. Disheartened, Talent looked at the mirror and saw the left part of his chest glowing. He entered his hands into his chest and pulled out the shining heart the beat of which stood for the pain he was enduring all these while. As he looked into the heart, he became enlightened since he realised that the empty heart can be filled only with passion. He understood that none of his hearts would be real unless he loves them. And it is the love for his heart that had caused the pain.(Here, heart stands for the skill of Talent.)

I know a lot of people who believe that they don't have a talent. To them, what I want to say is that there is always someone better than you in any field. You can never be the best until someone better than you doesn't show up. It's all relative.

Sometimes all you need is an Idea which is worth spreading.

If I try to give you a list of talents, it will go endless. What matters is not which talent you've got. It is how you use it and when you use it.

For example, if your talent lies in flirting, you can get all those techniques written in a book and help those with relationship issues and add a social value to it by saying that most relationships die because it gets boring and divorce cases are rocketing day by day.

If your talent lies in photography, you can take a photo album of the indigenous people who live in the deepest part of our country and showcase the album in a domain recognised by the public.

Similarly, it can be anything. It is your duty to think. I'm sure you will get an idea at the end of this chapter.

The talent which I have is in organising data and ideas in a way that is useful to others, and book is just a medium I'd selected to share it. Since I'm writing a book and have already written some, it won't be wrong if i call myself an author.

So, how did I identify my talent?

I'm also a Guitarist, but the method I used to identify my potential was to take the personality tests like 16personalitytests. Just Google it. Do it, and you'll get a clear idea of what you really are! But what helped me the most in finding my talents is whatever I chose; enjoy it like a talent.

Now, Our education system and society is programmed in such a way that we lose that spark and passion in us at a very early stage and we take a voyage to the field of science or money and by the time this realization hits, it would have become late. Maybe there are more things to realize.

If you want to make money, you don't have to know what your talent is. You can sell a bottle of water in a hot day and earn well.

But to identify that you have a talent and earn while doing something you love is something very important but is often forgotten. It is important because if we stop doing things we love for something else, you will end up hating yourself and the things you do will degrade you every damn second.

So, in order to avoid that and also keep your food supplies also available at the same time, at least start by adding the things you love during your work or studies. When you do that, you'll slowly gain expertise at a basic level in the things you love.

You're right, the passion you thought of while reading this is exactly what you should go for. With some creativity and tips from the 3rd Chapter, you'll be able to implement it.

PS: If you could think of nothing, think again. Maybe it's just the thing you are working or studying. You can make a Talent out of anything. If you still think the same way, just think about an activity you normally do. You are best at it if someone better than you isn't there.

Chapter 2: Talent Platform /Mountain of hearts

Finding a platform is easy, but finding the right platform suitable for you is the hardest part.

Why a platform is important is because, something is not recognised until it is in a place where everyone can watch and enjoy or look at when someone has a need.

You have to select a platform where you can flourish.

For example, if you are a 15-year- old boy and you go for a chess competition for those who are under 25 years, the chances are likely that you may not even be at the Top 10, except the fact that your experience level goes up. But let's be practical here. It's like a 2nd grade kid competing with a 10th grade boy in a quiz competition. He may lose. But if he wins, that's something. The only way for that to happen is either the boy should be very smart or the 10th std. boy should be very dumb.

So what I mean is that there are lots and lots of platforms where you can showcase your talent. But when you choose, choose to win with sufficient research and with careful observation. Because only that will make a difference. Don't forget that there's always someone better than you.

Meaning, at the end of the day, what matters is whether you win or not and what value you've shared with the world, and most importantly, whether you are satisfied or not.

What I did was to choose Amazon Kindle as my platform. Amazon kindle is one of the biggest online book services with 100s of books in each category. It's very user-friendly. So what Amazon Kindle does is when someone orders your book, it prints it on demand. Meaning, Amazon will print once someone orders a book.

You can create an e book or paperback as per your choice. As in the case of traditional publishing, your house will not become a book house and you can create content using just your phone. I don't have a PC. So I go to a café nearby and copy-paste whatever I've written on my note pad and edit there in Ms Word.

So, to write a book, what I needed was an account in kindle direct publishing. It's like signing into any service. Phone number, email ids and verification process, etc. You can design your cover and do everything so easily. You can also set it on presale and release it after one month. I did a whole book on Amazon kindle which made it to the Best Seller's List. Check it if you are really interested.

So, selecting a comfortable platform that you enjoy is the key here.

It's best to find credible platforms because only that can make your Talent credible. Search and find what's best for you. I recommend online platforms which are recognised.

And that's how, Talent reached the Mountain of Hearts where he had intended to keep his heart at its peak.

Chapter3: Do something Useful to the Society/City of Heartless.

When someone says of doing something useful to the society, it maybe misrepresented as something done for the sake of money. You don't have to buy anything or give some form of physical or financial help in order to do something useful.

So, what you can do with your talent need not be financial. It can be against a current social or political problem or for any movement or protest you think benefits our society rather than seeking to win a competition with it.

For example, if your talent is in drawing, or any sort of figure art, you can do grand figure regarding current social issues, and showcase it in a suitable credible platform.

So, there is a relationship between social issue and achievement. Greater the social issue and importance, lesser the achievement you need to be in Step 5.

I know we shouldn't be doing something expecting fame and status. I know that I can be criticised for this. But the truth is that if you want to be known and accepted by the world, do something useful with what you've got with you. It need not be free, because nobody values a free service until he/she is well-known. But if you feel so, you can do that also.

So, what I did is very controversial, since it is this book itself.

So, what I'm doing is helping people with no financial or political aid to be better known in your area of expertise by providing them with a path I believe is the map the beloved follower gave to Talent.

If you've got no money, we have to use the existing resources in an effective way.

PS: Even if you have achieved some recognition with your Talent, it won't be accepted until you help the people who don't care. That WILLINGNESS TO DO SOMETHING FOR PEOPLE WHO DON'T CARE ABOUT YOU MAKES YOU SPECIAL.

 Through this chapter, I want to convey that if a lot of people are get benefitted from you and others try to be their better versions, this world would be a much better place.

Talent shared most of his Heart to the City of heartless keeping only a small part for Fame, his love.

Chapter 4: Achieve Something

This is the most difficult but the easiest part at the same time.

What I did was to select a category with 100s of books, send a link to everyone on my Instagram following of about 2000 people.10 sales per day in a week will get someone to the best selling list. If I had chosen a different category, it would have taken 50 copies per day. So while choosing category I was very CAREFUL.I went through every possible category that was related to my last book and selected one from a category with more than 100 books but the contents were less competitive. I won't get the sales details until 90 days to know how many copies were sold. But I know who the audience is, that's the key. If you have a Talent, be clear who your audience will be or else you'll be singing nuclear physics to a dog. If you have a bone, go to a dog house to know its value. I had a book about Amazon Kindle which I shared in online book pages and groups. That maybe still circulating, since my book is still among the top 20.Only top 100 will be visible.

Disclaimer: If you are choosing my path, don't choose a category with only 10 books. You'll be #1 in no time, but when you approach media you'll suffer since they check every minor detail.

So what have you learnt so far from this? If you have a talent, spread it to the audience in online groups and pages just after you showcase it to the required platforms. Find out these online groups beforehand, so that you don't have to run when the time comes.

I had a very supportive family and a group of friends when I was writing my previous books. To achieve something, what you need the most is a reminder that helps you keep moving. For me, it was the essence of death itself. Life is too short to sit around and die one day. So get a legacy, get your name out there. Live the life that only a few can imagine. But there is a greater truth that even when you achieve something, it will not matter in the end. So, what would you choose, do nothing and die or be something and die? The "something" may differ from person to person and finally there will be something in each individual. Achieve it if you are curious to know what it feels like.

Our protagonist made it to the Top of the Mountain overcoming the rain and storm and he places his heart at its peak.

Step 5: Approaching the Media/Wield the Sword of Press

Legend says that only the worthy shall wield the sword of the Press. It was believed that the one who worked for others with his own ability selflessly and achieved greatness was worthy of the Press, until the emperor Nepotism took over the land of Press. Talent tries to wield the sword as he believes in the Legend of press.

Great! you have either done something useful to the society or achieved some recognition, or both. Now it's time that the world knows about it. Not in a big way but still in an effective way. Let's start slow.

What I did was search the list of all the online Malayalam news websites in Google. There were about 55 websites in that list. After I copy-pasted the list into my note pad, I searched for each website's contacts individually. Then I added their phone numbers and email ids also directly to the respective websites so that I can access them easily.

It is best to call directly or WhatsApp them rather than emailing, since I got no reply. I prepared what to say to them over and over again since I get stammered when I get overly nervous. Never forget to greet them and address them in a respectful way. It's important to say as little as possible and effectively. From my experience, it is better to inform them your name, place and age in the beginning. Then ask their name. Then comes the achievement/Useful deed and the key is to find similar news in the Internet, and tell them about it. I told them that there were similar news stories and that I thought that I can also be featured in the news or their website. So I called to the number given in the website. They would say that they'll let you be in contact with the respective reporter, and you'll have to explain to him everything in detail.

If you fail in that step, don't worry; you can go to the next reporter. If you reach out to 50 of them, I'm sure, at least 10 will respond positively, if you have a good story.

Now, Your Talent is in Media Outlet. Here comes the importance of platforms, so the readers, if they are interested in your talent, they may want to know where you've showcased your talent in order to see your other works.

This method is far more effective than someone showing their talent in social media, where the society does not value your talent. The only time when social media accepts your talent is when your talent is also accepted in mainstream media. That is, newspapers television etc.

The reason why so many extraordinary people are still not valued is that they are not willing to get out of their most comfortable platforms like instagram, tiktok, Facebook, YouTube, twitter etc. I may be criticised for adding tiktok to this list. But if you look closely, are the personalities famous in any of these platforms valued in any mainstream news or formally recognised in society? Yes, some of those who have verified badges in these platforms just because they were in the mainstream media.

So, instead of aiming for presenting your talent in social media, the best way is to aim for formal mainstream news or their online websites and slingshot back to where you are comfortable in while also working on the credible platform that helped you to get into the mainstream media.

I have experienced only the things up to the step in which I approached an online news website and they said yes.

The steps to slingshot back to social media will be written in the Part 2 after Talent wields the sword of press, and when the people of Press believes in Him.

I believe that I don't have the right to write about something I have not experienced. So I hope to release a sequel to this book very soon and inspire young talents. Thank you.

<u>REFERENCE</u>

"सर्वे: हाईकोर्ट के 50 और सुप्रीम कोर्ट के 33% जज चंद घरानों के बेटे-भतीजे, भारत में ज्यूडिशरी का हाल". जनसत्ता. जनसत्ता. 26 April 2020.

"'Nepotism' in Collegium System, Alleges Allahabad HC Judge in Fawning Letter to Modi". The Wire. 4 July 2019.

"Govt gives collegium 'proof' of nepotism in picks for HC judges". The Times of India. 1 August 2018.

"Who's the Judge?". The Statesman. 21 September 2016.

"Check complaints of judges' children clearing judicial exam: Sadananda Gowda asks Chief Justice". The Indian Express. 26 June 2015.

"The family connections of India Inc".

https://thewire.in/politics/bjp-congress-political-dynasties-lok-sabha

"Across India, Nepotism as a Way of Life". International Herald Tribune. 12 April 2012 – via The New York Times.

"Nepotism: the way they do politics in India". The Sydney Morning Herald. 27 March 2014.

https://www.huffingtonpost.in/entry/amit-shah-jay-shah-new-bcci-secretary-twitter_in_5da413fde4b06ddfc51ca11c